Overview *My Sand Pie*

A boy uses many tools to make a sand pie.

Reading Vocabulary Words

bucket
shovel
plate

High-Frequency Words

my	goes
here	go
is	look
the	at

Building Future Vocabulary

These vocabulary words do not appear in this text. They are provided to develop related oral vocabulary that first appears in future texts.

Words:	*yard*	*add*	*hat*
Levels:	Turquoise	Turquoise	Yellow

Comprehension Strategy
Recognizing cause and effect

Fluency Skill
Falling voice at end of declarative sentences

Phonics Skill
Initial sounds: letter *h* (<u>h</u>ere)

Reading-Writing Connection
Listing the steps in a process

... .ie Flying
...lake-Home books for children to share with their families.

Differentiated Instruction
Before reading the text, query children to discover their level of understanding of the comprehension strategy — Recognizing cause and effect. As you work together, provide additional support to children who show a beginning mastery of the strategy.

Focus on ELL

- Give children two containers of sand. Add water to one and keep the other dry. Use the wet sand to form a shape. Try the same with the dry sand. Discuss the difference.

- Ask children where sand is found. (beach, playground)

Using This Teaching Version

1. Before Reading

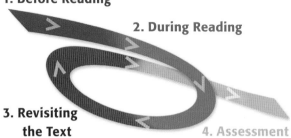

2. During Reading

3. Revisiting the Text

4. Assessment

This Teaching Version will assist you in directing children through the process of reading.

1. **Begin with Before Reading** to familiarize children with the book's content. Select the skills and strategies that meet the needs of your children.

2. **Next, go to During Reading** to help children become familiar with the text, and then to read individually on their own.

3. **Then, go back to Revisiting the Text** and select those specific activities that meet children's needs.

4. Finally, finish with Assessment to confirm children are ready to move forward to the next text.

---

1 Before Reading

Building Background

- Write the word *bucket* on the board. Point to the word as you read it aloud. What does a bucket help us do? (hold or carry things)

- Introduce the book by reading the title, talking about the cover photograph, and sharing the overview.

Building Future Vocabulary
Use Interactive Modeling Card: Word Web

- Introduce the word *yard*. Tell children that a yard is where children play. Write the word *yard* in the center of the Word Web.

- Ask children to name play items that may be found in a yard, such as a sandbox and swings. List each item on the Word Web.

Introduction to Reading Vocabulary

- On blank cards write: *bucket*, *shovel*, and *plate*. Read them aloud. Tell children these words will appear in the text of *My Sand Pie*.

- Use each word in a sentence for understanding.

Introduction to Comprehension Strategy

Use Interactive Modeling Card: Questions and Answers Chart

- Explain that when one thing happens (a cause), it can make another thing happen (an effect).

- Together read the title *My Sand Pie*. Ask children to think of questions about the cover photograph that may be answered after reading the story, such as *Why is the boy wearing a hat? How will he make the pie? Will he eat the pie?* List children's questions on the Questions and Answers Chart. Be sure to include questions that may have a cause-and-effect relationship.

Introduction to Phonics

- Write on the board: **here**. Read the word aloud. Point to the letter *h*. Tell children that **here** begins with the letter *h*. Model for them that the letter *h* sounds like /h/.

- Together read the sentence on page 2. Have children point to the word **here**.

- Have children look for the word **here** as they read *My Sand Pie*.

Modeling Fluency

- Read aloud page 2, modeling the falling voice at the end of a declarative sentence.

- Point to the period. Explain that the use of a period at the end of a statement tells the reader to stop. Also explain that when you read a sentence that ends in a period, your voice should fall at the end of it.

2 During Reading

Book Talk

Beginning on page T4, use the During Reading notes on the left-hand side to engage children in a book talk. On page 16, follow with Individual Reading.

Book Talk

- Tell children that some books explain how to do something. They are often called "how-to" books. Ask *What will this book tell you how to do?* (make a sand pie)

- Discuss the title page photograph. Ask children to predict how the boy will use each tool to make the sand pie.

- **Comprehension Strategy** Ask *Why is the boy adding stones to his sand pie?* (to make it look like a real pie)

Turn to page 2 — Book Talk

My Sand Pie

Future Vocabulary

• Have children look at the cover photograph. Ask *What clues tell us that this story takes place in a yard?* (There is a fence behind the boy that looks like a yard-type fence. There are planted flowers that look like those planted in a yard.)

• Ask children to share what they have in their yards at home. Ask *Do you have a sandbox, too?*

Now revisit pages 2–3

1

Book Talk

- Ask *What is the first thing the boy does to make his sand pie?* (picks up his bucket)

- Have children locate the word *bucket* on page 2. Ask children to find the picture of the bucket on page 3. Ask *What is another name for a bucket?* (pail)

Turn to page 4 – Book Talk

Here is the bucket.

2

Future Vocabulary

- Show children a yardstick and explain different meanings of the word *yard*. Say *A yard is a place to play at a person's house, but it is also a measurement of the length or height of an object.* Explain that a yard is three feet long. Spread your arms out and tell children that three feet is about the length between your hands.

- Have children predict whether they are taller or shorter than a yard. Measure volunteers to check their predictions.

Now revisit pages 4–5

During Reading

Book Talk

- Ask *Does the boy like playing in the sand?* (yes) *How can you tell?* (He is smiling.)

- Have children locate the word *shovel* on page 4. Ask children to point to the shovel in the picture on page 5.

Turn to page 6 — Book Talk

Here is the shovel.

4

4

Future Vocabulary

- Have children look at page 5 and find the bucket. Ask *Is the bucket longer or shorter than a yard?* (shorter) *Is the shovel longer or shorter than a yard?* (shorter) *Is the boy taller or shorter than a yard?* (probably taller but we cannot tell because he is sitting)

Now revisit pages 6–7

Book Talk

- Ask *What does the boy use the shovel to do?* (scoop sand into the bucket) *What are some other things the boy could use to scoop the sand into the bucket?* (spoon, hands, cup)

- **Comprehension Strategy** Ask *If the boy poured too much sand in his bucket, what would happen?* (The bucket would overflow.) *The cause is pouring too much sand, and the effect is that the bucket overflows.*

Turn to page 8 – Book Talk

Here is the sand.

6

Future Vocabulary

- Ask children to look at page 7. Say *The boy is wearing a blue hat. What color is your favorite hat?* List responses as tally marks on the board.

- Ask *What other kinds of hats do people wear?* (baseball hat/cap, hard hat, ski hat, police/fire hat) *Why do people wear hats?* (to protect their heads from sun, cold, or injury)

Now revisit pages 8–9

Book Talk

- **Comprehension Strategy** Ask *What will happen to the sand now that the boy has added water?* (It will hold its shape.) *Adding water causes the sand to hold its shape. What will happen if the boy packs the sand down and turns the bucket over?* (The sand will come out in the shape of the bucket.)

- **Phonics Skill** Have children locate the word *here* on page 8. Remind them that *here* begins with the letter *h*, which sounds like /h/.

Turn to page 10 — Book Talk

Here is the water.

8

Future Vocabulary

- Hold a hat in your hand. Ask *How long will it take for the hat to fall to the floor?* (a short time) *Is it hard or easy to drop a hat?* (easy)

- Tell children that another way to use the word *hat* is in the expression "drop of a hat." Ask *Do you think this means "a long time" or "a short time"?* (a short time)

- Use the expression in a sentence. Say *The boy was ready to go to the park at the drop of a hat.*

Now revisit pages 10–11

Book Talk

- Ask *What is made in a* plate *like this one?* (pie) *How is a pie* plate *different from a dinner* plate? (A dinner plate is flat or almost flat all around. A pie plate has higher sides for the crust.)

- Have children locate the word *plate* on this page. Ask *What sound begins the word* plate? (/p/)

Turn to page 12 – Book Talk

Here   is   the   plate.

10

Future Vocabulary

- **Phonics Skill** Ask *What sound do you hear at the beginning of the word* hat? *(/h/) Which word on this page also begins with /h/? (here) What letter has that sound? (h)*

Now revisit pages 12–13

During Reading

Book Talk

- Ask *How did the boy get the sand from the bucket to the plate?* (with a spoon) *What might have happened if he had tried to pour the sand into the plate?* (It would not pour out easily because it was wet, or it would have overflowed the pie plate.)

- **Phonics Skill** Have children locate the word *here* on this page.

Turn to page 14 – Book Talk

The sand goes here.

12

Future Vocabulary

- Ask *What is the boy doing?* (putting sand into the plate or adding sand to the plate)

- Ask *What would the boy do if he did not have enough sand in the plate?* (He would add more.)

- To add can also mean to find the number of something. Ask children to add the number of tools in the photograph.

Now revisit pages 14–15

During Reading

Book Talk

- Ask *What colors are the leaves the boy has put on the sand pie?* (red, green, and orange) *Where do you think the boy got the leaves?* (from plants in his yard) *What kind of plants do you usually find in a yard?* (flowers, leafy plants, bushes, garden fruits and vegetables)

- **Fluency Skill** Have children locate the period at the end of the sentence. Remind them that a period shows the end of a statement.

Turn to page 16 – Book Talk

The leaves go here.

14

Future Vocabulary

- Discuss items that may be found in a yard such as flowers, fruits and vegetables, rocks, and so on.

- Together reread page 14. Say *The boy adds things to decorate his sand pie. What things would you add to decorate your own sand pie?*

Go to page T5 —
Revisiting the Text

During Reading

Book Talk

- Leave this page for children to discover on their own when they read the book individually.

Individual Reading

Have each child read the entire book at his or her own pace while remaining in the group.

Go to page T5 – Revisiting the Text

Look at my sand pie.

16

During independent work time, children can read the online book at:

www.rigbyflyingcolors.com

Revisiting the Text

Future Vocabulary

- Use the notes on the right-hand pages to develop oral vocabulary that goes beyond the text. These vocabulary words first appear in future texts. These words are: *yard*, *add*, and *hat*.

Turn back to page 1

Reading Vocabulary Review
Activity Sheet: Word Web

- Write these words in squares on the Word Web: *bucket*, *shovel*, and *plate*.

- Write *tools* in the circle. Say *The boy used tools.* Help children complete the Word Web with other tools.

Comprehension Strategy Review
Use Interactive Modeling Card: Questions and Answers Chart

- Discuss *My Sand Pie*. Reread each question on the chart. Write children's answers on the card.

- Point out the questions related to cause and effect, such as *Why is the boy wearing a hat?* (because of the hot sun) or *Will he eat the pie?* (no, because it might make him sick)

Phonics Review

- Have children look through the book to find examples of **Here** and **here**.

- Brainstorm a list of words that begin with *h*. Say sentences with these words and have children raise their hands when they hear an initial /h/.

Fluency Review

- Have children turn to page 16. Point out the period and remind children that it is the end of a sentence. Together, read the sentence aloud to practice how a voice falls at a period.

- Read aloud the entire book. Have children hold out their hands and say "Stop!" at the end of each sentence.

Reading-Writing Connection
Activity Sheet: Questions and Answers Chart

To assist children with linking reading and writing:

- Help children ask questions about which tools the boy used first, second, and so on.

- Have children refer to the text and answer the questions with words or pictures. Together read each tool the boy used. Have children number the tools.

T5

Assessing Future Vocabulary

Work with each child individually. Ask questions that elicit each child's understanding of the Future Vocabulary words. Note each child's responses:

- What is a yard? Tell another meaning for the word *yard*.
- What types of hats do people wear? What does "drop of a hat" mean?
- What did the boy add to the sand to make his sand pie?

Assessing Comprehension Strategy

Work with each child individually. Note each child's understanding of cause and effect:

- What caused the boy to wear a hat?
- What was the effect of the water on the sand?
- The boy added leaves to the sand pie. What effect did this have on the pie?
- Was each child able to tell you the cause and effect of each event?

Assessing Phonics

Work with each child individually. Note each child's responses for understanding words beginning with /h/. Show words beginning with *h*. Have children point to the letter *h* in each word:

- Give each child a letter card for *h*. Say the following words and have each child hold up the card when they hear an initial /h/: *horse, cow, pig, hog, hand, head, foot, heart, jump, hop, hot,* and *hurt.*
- Did each child understand the letter-sound correspondence between *h* and /h/?

Assessing Fluency

Have each child read page 2 to you. Note each child's understanding of how a voice falls at the end of a declarative sentence:

- Was each child able to accurately read the sentence?
- Was each child able to make their voice fall at the end of the sentence?
- Was each child able to identify the period as a stopping point?

Interactive Modeling Cards

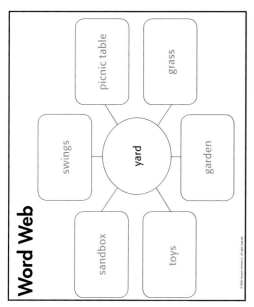

Word Web

Directions: With children, fill in the Word Web using the word *yard*.

Questions and Answers Chart

Title *My Sand Pie*

Topic Making something

Questions	Answers
Why is the boy wearing a hat?	It is sunny.
How will he make the pie?	He will use different tools.
Will he eat the pie?	He will not eat it because it is not food.
Why is the boy smiling?	He is happy because he made something.
Will anyone help him?	No, he made the pie by himself.
Why does the boy have a bucket?	It helped him make the sand pie.

Directions: With children, fill in the Questions and Answers Chart for *My Sand Pie*.

Discussion Questions

- What items or tools did the boy use to make his sand pie? (Literal)
- What would have happened if there had been no water to wet the sand? (Critical Thinking)
- Will the boy enjoy making other things from sand? What might he like to make? (Inferential)

Activity Sheets

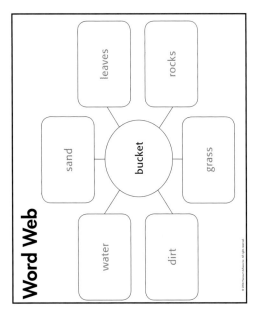

Word Web

leaves

rocks

sand

bucket

grass

water

dirt

Directions: Have children fill in the Word Web using the word *bucket* in the center oval. Have children write items that may be carried in a bucket.

Questions and Answers Chart

Title **My Sand Pie**

Topic **Making something**

Questions	Answers
What tool did the boy use first?	bucket
What tool did he use next?	shovel
Then what tool did he use?	plate
What tool did he use last?	spoon

Directions: Have children fill in the Questions and Answers Chart and use their answers to make a list of the tools the boy used.
Optional: Have children read their questions and answers aloud.